The SALVATION

Eugene Lawrance Webb

outskirts
press

The Meaning of Salvation
All Rights Reserved.
Copyright © 2023 Eugene Lawrance Webb
v2.0

The opinions expressed in this manuscript are solely the opinions of the author and do not represent the opinions or thoughts of the publisher. The author has represented and warranted full ownership and/or legal right to publish all the materials in this book.

This book may not be reproduced, transmitted, or stored in whole or in part by any means, including graphic, electronic, or mechanical without the express written consent of the publisher except in the case of brief quotations embodied in critical articles and reviews.

Outskirts Press, Inc.
http://www.outskirtspress.com

ISBN: 978-1-9772-6088-8

Cover Photo © 2023 www.gettyimages.com. All rights reserved - used with permission.

Outskirts Press and the "OP" logo are trademarks belonging to Outskirts Press, Inc.

PRINTED IN THE UNITED STATES OF AMERICA

Table of Contents

Preface	i
1 God IS	1
2 Before Time	7
3 The First Adam	13
4 The Garden of Eden; Deception	19
5 The Remnant	25
6 Working for Our Good	31
7 Keys to His Purpose	37
8 End Times	43
9 Conclusion	51

Preface

In this book, you will discover a slightly different view on the normal paradigm of standard Christian religious belief according to the dogmas of the day. The first thing you have to understand is the essence of God. He is immense, larger than the universe, creation, and our known existence! God transcends space, time, and dimensions; the only one to actually see God the Father is Jesus the Son (John 1:38). The creator of all things is everywhere at the same time, throughout all time. This is how God knows and controls everything because He is at the beginning and end of time simultaneously. God the Father knew what was going to happen when He created the angels and man. Seeing all things, God still chose to make man because of His great love and mercy, orchestrating salvation before man was ever created (Psalm 139:14).

God has orchestrated salvation since before time. God is Omniscient, Omnipotent, and Omnipresent, which means He knows everything that will ever happen. That's why He allowed the enemy to stay free for a time because He knew how to use the enemies' hatred for good (Romans 8:28)! Satan didn't want to serve God anymore and rebelled, but he still does, only in a fallen and disgraced condition. If you have found faith in Jesus, it is because He first called you and had you find your way to Him. Hallelujah!

This book will give you a fresh look at old faithful truths and help you understand how much God truly loves us and what He was willing to endure for that love. You will see the great intellect of God and how no one can outwit Him, especially the Enemy. Always have your trust in God; no matter what is happening, know God is in control (Romans 13:1)!

Chapter One

GOD IS

TO UNDERSTAND AND absorb the knowledge in this book, we first have to look at the attributes of God himself. According to the normal Christian dogma, God is omnipresent, omnipotent, and omniscient, but exactly what does that mean? You must try to see God the way the Holy Bible describes him and understand what that means if you follow it out to its logical end (Proverbs 15:3). Simply put, God is everywhere at the same time, throughout all time! As simple as that is to say, wrapping our human understanding around exactly what that means can be difficult, because we are only humans with limited knowledge. God has always been, is, and always will be unmovable and unchanging. He is the ultimate righteousness, holiness, full of mercy and love. But I think He is at the beginning of time and at the end of time simultaneously, allowing him to know everything, which gives him the ability to control everything. God's only limitations are those He imposes on himself in order to give us free will. Understand that God knew a third of the angels would rebel before He created them, but He used that knowledge for good when He created man. People have wondered why God allowed the enemy to roam free instead of sending them all straight to Hell, which He prepared for them. God's intellect is so far above everyone else's that it cannot even be measured (Isaiah 55:9)! Even the highest angels cannot come close to God's intelligence, especially the enemy, which God runs circles around. Lucifer fell because he did not want to serve God; he even believed he was better than God. Whatever God sets out to do, it will be done, and nothing can stop it (Isaiah 55:11)! In his fallen and disgraced state, Satan, as Lucifer is now called, which means "the enemy," still serves God's purposes because God is so clever that He uses the enemies' actions for evil and turns them around for good for those who love God (Romans 8:28). That is why God allowed Satan to roam free until He was finished with him, and then He would throw all of the fallen into Hell. That is the advantage of knowing everything that is ever going to happen: you can manage actions in time any way that you choose. Some might choose to call that predestination, but it really is not. God gives us free will, which is the one control He gives up to us; just because He knows already what we will choose does not mean that is predestination. God is the best at thinking outside the box and can have twists and turns that no one will see coming, not even the angels. That's why Satan's evil actions against humanity failed because God outsmarted him by using those actions to bring about salvation for the remnant that would be willing to follow God.

God is wonderfully good, compassionate, just, and He shows mercy to those that repent. As Jesus stated, "If you have seen Me, you have seen the Father" (John 14:8-10), and He despised hypocrisy, legalism, corruption, lying, indifference, cruelty, and especially pride. Jesus loved to see people who were faithful, showed mercy, had honesty, were truthful and compassionate, and showed kindness with humility. These are the things He praised. God's plans are always to help us for good and to give us hope (Jeremiah 29:11). God is bigger than the entire created universe, time, space, or dimensions. He is limitless and larger than anything we can imagine. From our point of view, God is in the past, present, and future simultaneously; therefore, God is everywhere across existence in terms of times and dimensions. God is outside of space and time and has no beginning, end, or succession of moments in his own being. He is outside of our known existence, beyond anything we can conceive of in our minds, and only Jesus has seen the Father (John 6:46). The infinity of God includes both his eternity and his immensity; God's transcendence means that he is outside space and time and therefore eternal and unable to be changed by forces within the universe. Taking that into account, that means he knows every sin we have committed, are committing, and will commit, but still he loves us and gave his life for us. God's loving nature is equally perplexing; why would the Creator love us so much, but we are grateful he does? Praise our Holy God, from whom all blessings flow, and praise His name for all eternity (1st Kings 8:27; Psalm 90:2; 139:8; Isaiah 40:28; 57:15; John 3:16; 1st John 4:16)!

In the beginning, God created the universe for the existence of humankind. The universe contains certain laws that God created to limit our physical and temporal existence here in this world, which does not transcend to the real world of the celestial. Reality is the celestial world, of which we have no concept of the physics. God is much bigger than most people think. God, like a small model, holds the universe in His hand. God is ever present, all knowing, and exists outside of time, which is only limited to our universe. This knowledge makes me in awe of God's wondrous love, that He would be mindful of us!

God is spirit (John 4:4, Colossians 1:15, 1st Timothy 1:17) and far above anything we can imagine or conceive. From our point of view, God is the perfect balance between masculine and feminine attributes working together in perfect harmony. This reminds me of the Ying and Yang symbol that the Asians have, which shows perfect harmony between the elements of light and darkness. Everything God has created is perfectly structured and moves in perfect logical order, for God is the balance of the universe. That is why everything in the universe is in perfect logical order, which did not happen from a big bang, and from chaos came perfect composition. How ridiculous are some of the scientists who simply refuse to believe in God? Those who are familiar with the Bible may refer to scriptures that say God had a physical presence, such as with Abraham (Genesis 18:23-33) and Moses (Exodus 33:17-23), but those were points where Jesus took physical form to meet with people. God has always been and will always be; that's why God used the famous "I am that I Am" statement (Exodus 3:14), and God is the Eternal God of all (Isaiah 40:28, Revelation 1:8). The Trinity has always been with God, even from the beginning, as Jesus is the living Word of God (John 1:1-5) and the Holy Spirit is the spirit that moved over the face of the waters in the Old Testament (Genesis 1:2). God is a God of Love, and He brings Salvation to all who are lost and acknowledge their need for God's forgiveness.

Only through God's provision of Jesus the Christ and the sacrifice He made for us can we be saved by Faith. Jesus took on all of the human race's sins from the beginning to the end and paid the price so that none of us would have to die. The only sin you now go to hell for is called "the blasphemy of the Holy Spirit" (Matthew 12:31; Mark 3:28-29; 12:10; Hebrews 10:26-29), which means denying Jesus as your Lord and Savior! The Holy Spirit's main emphasis is to edify Jesus as the Christ; denying that is unforgiveable! If anyone goes to Hell now, they can only blame themselves because God has done everything he can to make the way for us. God loves to redeem the lost, which is a recurring theme throughout the Old and New Testaments. Nevertheless, it does state in the Scriptures that in the end, everyone will bow their knee and confess that Jesus is the Lord and Savior (Philippians 2:10-11).

Chapter Two

BEFORE TIME

Now that we have a clearer view of God, you can understand how nothing could catch God by surprise, and people who think God has been caught off guard just do not know Him. God is more ingenious than any organism alive and does use all things to bring Himself glory, no matter the circumstances. This is what makes God's salvation plan (Isaiah 12) so amazing that even the angels of God stand in wonderment! With God's intricate plan of salvation, He sees all and, with perceptive anticipation, can adjust future events to match His plan. When Lucifer rebelled against God, it was no surprise; God mentions Satan's breach of sin (Ezekiel 28:15). Lucifer became Satan, which means "the enemy," and his fall is recorded in **Isaiah 14** and **Ezekiel 28,** which describe how his pride, vanity, and greed led to his destruction.

Satan was thrown out of heaven with a great fall, and his anger was focused on the inhabitants of Earth (Revelation 12:7-12). Satan has always been jealous for the loss of his reign on Earth after he tried to ascend to heaven and take it from God, but he lost the battle and his position with God. In Ezekiel 28:15-19, it is actually speaking of Satan in the duality reference sometimes used in the Holy Bible. In Isaiah 14:12-17 it describes how he was created perfect but, he chose to sin and God cast him down. Lucifer, who before his fall was known as the "Son of the Morning" and ruled over the kingdoms of the old earth, which were ruled by angels, this time was way before man existed, and there were kingdoms, principalities, and powers that Lucifer had rule over until the fall, when God flooded the whole earth for the first time (Genesis 1:2). After that, the earth was formless and empty, and darkness covered the whole earth because of the judgment of God against Satan's rebellion.

This was the first flood, and a lot of people get this one mixed up with the Noah flood, which happened much later after Adam came to be. Peter talks about this in 2nd Peter 3:6-7, pointing out the "**Ancient World,**" which would be when Lucifer ruled the Earth, and the "**Present Heaven and Earth,**" which is the world we live in now. This is the little blurb in Genesis 1:2 that most people skip over and don't realize it is about the first total destruction of Earth. During the Lucifer flood, everything was destroyed; it was an empty void. In Ezekiel 28:11-19, it goes over the fall of Lucifer, where he becomes Satan, and the destruction he brought to the Earth at that time. The Garden of God in verse 13 is not the Garden of Eden but a different garden at the time of the first flood. Jesus created everything because He is the Living Word of God (Colossians 1:15-20), which includes all of the visible and unseen thrones, kingdoms, rulers, and authorities. Lucifer was one of the rulers of Earth before he fell and was made perfect with great beauty. The story of the angels who sinned and God did not spare judgment is told in 2nd Peter 2:4. If one thinks about all the things that science and archaeology have uncovered, like the megalithic structures around the world that we can't build even today. Angels would have no problem building with those gigantic stones and with the precision they were put together with, so you could not even get a piece of paper between the stones. Also, it mentions in 2nd Corinthians 4:4 that Satan is the god of this world and blinds people to the truth about Jesus. The enemy is called by many names: serpent, dragon, prince of devils, tempter, unclean spirit, and wicked one. His titles give you an idea of his goal for the people of this world. Speaking of the end times, it is said to have seducing spirits and doctrines of devils (John 12:31), which match the world we live in now. In John 8:44, it talks about people who love to do what Satan does because they are his children.

With the previous civilization mentioned in the Bible, after the creation of everything, Earth was without form or void, how could God have already created everything? God destroyed the Earth the second time by Flood which wiped out the fallen earthbound ones, the Nephilim. This is after God created man and woman and began again, which is why God promised Noah that the earth would never be destroyed by flood again. This previous civilization during the time of Lucifer's reign on Earth might have had humanoid people, which could explain the Neanderthals. The Neanderthals could have been normal humans, but they were so corrupted by sin that they became more like animals?

Even in the Old Testament, there were numerous references to giants known as Nephilim (Numbers 13:33) or by other names such as Amorites (Amos 2:9), Anakites (Deuteronomy 1:28, 2:10-11, 21, 9:2, Joshua 11:21-22, 14:12-14), Emites (Genesis 14:6, Deuteronomy 2:10), Zamzummim (Deuteronomy 2:20, Joshua 2:10), and Rephaim. The Watchers were the offspring of human women and fallen angels of God (Enoch 7:2-6, Jude 1:6). These creatures were known to be completely evil, but strong and knowledgeable for their time. God always rained down judgment on anyone who accepted an alliance with the Earth-bound Fallen Ones (Nephilim), which is why Sodom and Gomorrah were destroyed because of their desire for "strange flesh" (Genesis 18:20, Romans 1:18-32, 2nd Timothy 4:8, Jude 1:7).

People wondered why God would allow Satan to roam free instead of throwing him straight into the hell that was prepared for him. Remember, God can use all things to bring glory to Himself (Romans 8:28). Even the evil plans Satan means to do harm, God can turn around for His glory. Satan didn't sneak into the Garden of Eden under God's radar; God let him in to help fulfill His own purposes. God knows the thoughts of everyone and knew Satan wanted revenge for being cast out, and man seemed to be an easy target. It would be conjecture to say that Adam, left alone, would have fallen on his own anyway, but Satan's impatience hatched the plan to bring man down. God allowed Satan to act out his hatred, wanting to destroy in order to save the remnant of humanity that would accept God's ways. The law of sin is death, which is absolute, but the loophole in that law is that if you are tricked into sinning, you can be bought back. This is why God allowed Satan to enter the Garden of Eden and tempt man to fall so that God could buy us back. God is a redemptive God, and with His great love, He never fails to redeem. Jesus was willing to do God's will in order to buy back man (Acts 4:12), saving those whom God had given him, as recorded in the Book of Life in Heaven (Revelation 3:5).

As you will see, this is the essence of the whole plan of salvation that God has planned since the beginning of time. God is the Alpha and the Omega, the beginning and the end; He knows everything that will ever happen and controls the same. The intricate interweaving of the plan of salvation could only be done by God because it is beyond our ability to comprehend all of the twists put into place, and this was done on purpose to keep the enemy from guessing what God was doing. God is now opening up revelations to His great plans as we get nearer to the end of the time of the gentiles, just before the last week of Daniel, and this will complete everything, which I will discuss further in another chapter.

Chapter Three

THE FIRST ADAM

As you can see from the earlier chapter, we have an enemy that will stop at nothing to see the destruction of all humankind just because of his jealousy. In the book of Genesis, the first chapter, verses 26 and 27, it talks about how God made Adam in His own image. Further, God said He made Adam from the dust of the ground and breathed life into him (Genesis 2:7, 1st Corinthians 15:45). God made Adam in His image, but a lot of people miss the significance of that statement. Later on, in chapter two of Genesis, you see God create a mate for Adam and take a part of him to form his spouse (Genesis 2:21). That word translated from ancient Hebrew, "rib," has three different meanings. One definition is the rib of a boat, which has the connotation of being inanimate. The second definition is a cube or cell, but the connotation here is still inanimate. Some theologians speculate that could mean blood cells, but why would God have to put Adam in a deep sleep to draw blood (Genesis 2:21)? This simply does not make any sense, but there was a definition that was animate and not used. The third definition, which did have an animate connotation and was human-related, was not used in the translation, probably because their machoism could not handle it. The term "womb" leads us to believe that Adam's first construction was self-reproducing because God does not require assistance. Before you dismiss the idea, think of all the representations you have seen of angels. They have a feminine look, but all of them have male names.

Then again, the word "woman," if you read right to left as they do in the Eastern areas, is "man with womb," and this is a more accurate statement. Jesus also stated in the gospel of Luke, chapter 20, verses 34-36, that we will have bodies like the angels have in heaven and there will be no marriage there except the marriage of the lamb. This would be a better explanation of where the daughters came from to marry the sons of Eve than some of the other discussions I have heard. Adam was around for some time before Eve was fashioned because Adam had enough time to name all the animals in the world which would have taken some time to do (Genesis 2:19). There is no accurate account of Adam's true age except after Eve was formed; that's when Adam's age was counted (Genesis 5:5).

Now that God put Adam into a deep sleep to remove part of him, he must have also changed Adam's genetic structure so he would only reproduce with a single sex. Science tells us that human babies are predisposed to be female, with the exception of the **Y chromosome,** which will make the baby a boy. Men probably strive to make their mark in the world because Adam gave up the ability to create life in order to have a spouse. An interesting note about Eve being "fashioned" from Adam is that the Hebrew term "fashioned" is where we get the word "artwork." So, if you extend the logical application of that, Eve was God's artwork, and there is no need to try to improve on that with makeup because God made women naturally beautiful. When Eve was fashioned from Adam, God also separated the elements of personality that would allow each to do their jobs. We call this "masculine" and "feminine" because Adam was originally self-reproducing, just like God. That is why the Scriptures refer to marriage between man and woman as "becoming one flesh" because the elements are reunited (Genesis 2:24). In our fallen states of sin, it is nearly impossible to get the perfect harmonious balance between the masculine and feminine in our marriages like God originally wanted. Sin is the most destructive force in the universe because it destroys everything down to its smallest element. The invading nature of sin will saturate every component and contaminate everything good until it becomes depraved. God made angels perfect, and if sin can absolutely destroy a high-level angel like Lucifer, then you can understand its immense power.

In reference to Jesus' statement about binding the strongman (Matthew 12:29; Mark 3:27; Luke 11:21-22) first before you can take the house, this refers to the dominions, principalities, powers, and rulers of darkness. The enemy has its own hierarchy to combat the faithful in this world, just like an army has generals, colonels, captains, and lieutenants that are assigned duties to fight their enemy.

We must comprehend the resolve of our enemy in order to counter their attacks against the faithful. Every military commander realizes that you must know your enemy and their tactics to come up with a strategy in your life to defeat them. The reader needs to see the enemy clearly and his goals against the church, which will help him recognize the attacks and their manifestations. Knowing your enemy means you will know how to mount an effective counterattack, stopping their fiery darts and fighting them with a winning plan to overcome and defeat them.

God gives us nine gifts of the Holy Spirit, which are broken up into three groups: <u>discerning gifts</u>, <u>declarative gifts,</u> and <u>dynamic gifts,</u> to help the faithful overcome the attacks of the enemy.

The enemy has dark spirits mentioned in the Bible, broken up into three hierarchies to counter the gifts of the Holy Spirit. These groups tempt humankind to sin through <u>irrationalism</u>, <u>confusion,</u> and <u>indifference,</u> which are attacks on the flesh, mind, and human spirit. These dark spirits have one goal in mind, and that is to destroy all believers and non-believers alike (1st Peter 5:8).

The reader must prepare themselves and overcome our enemy by using God's provisions in combat with the enemy of this world so people can be saved, healed, and set free. Bless the holy name of Jesus, the risen Son of God and savior of the world.

When I say sin destroys everything at every level, this includes intelligence because sin makes people absolutely stupid. Sin distorts common sense and corrupts even the most extraordinary intellect. That is why Saint Paul tells us in Ephesians to put on all of God's armor because we are in a desperate battle for our very souls (Ephesians 6:12-18). Paul challenges us to live as children of light through the changing of our lifestyles and putting off our old sinful natures (Ephesians 4:17-24). We are told to fix our thoughts on the good things of God and what we have been taught about His nature (Philippians 4:8). But if we do sin, we have an advocate who will defend us because of His love for us before the father (1st Timothy 2:5-6).

Chapter Four

THE GARDEN OF EDEN; DECEPTION

YOU NEED TO understand the intent of the garden's purpose, which is to fulfill God's direction and His will for humanity. I have briefly mentioned earlier how God allowed Satan to enter the garden to tempt humankind to activate the loophole in the law of sin is death. This allowed God to buy us back and simultaneously separate the wheat from the chaff (Matthew 3:12). God gives us free will, and that is why He allowed this to happen so the true followers would come to God willingly. God did not want automatons; He only wanted those who would willingly love God and follow His ways. According to the scriptures, God knows us before we are even born, which is to say, God knows everything (Jeremiah 1:5).

As Jesus pointed out, God looks at the heart of a person (Jeremiah 17:10, Romans 8:27, Acts 15:8, Hebrews 4:12) and searches out all our intentions to know our motivations.

Even though Satan deceived Adam and Eve, he was duped by God by allowing him to enter the garden in the first place. Satan foolishly thought he outsmarted God, which shows his level of self-deception in thinking he could do that. The stage was set so that flesh and gender would be a weak stance for humanity, making them an easy target. Adam brought death to the world of humanity, but the second Adam, namely Jesus, brought life and redemption. There are many references where Jesus is referred to as the aspect of life: living water (John 4:10), bread of life (John 6:35), advocate (1st John 2:1), the resurrection (John 11:25), and the way, truth, and life (John 14:6), etc. This is God's nature to redeem what is lost through His great love and mercies. The wonderous mercy and grace only extended to the human race because when the watchers fell, they were lost forever (Enoch chapters 6-7). Those were the 200 angel watchers that fell because of their lust for women (Genesis 6:1-4), and this was the second fall of angels. We do not have an exact time when the fall of Lucifer happened; we just know it was before Adam was created. Reading in the Book of Enoch, you can see they knew it was going to cost them their relationship with God, but they still went through with it.

They had to give up their celestial bodies (Oiketerion) to be able to produce children; what could have possessed them just to be intimate with human women to produce children (Jude 1:6)?

You can see how dangerous sin is when it can take out angels of God multiple times. As I have said before, sin is the most corruptible action that has long-reaching effects that never seem to end as it destroys everything. Sin is more corrosive than the most potent acids, more destructive than a nuclear bomb, and it perverts everything to its most putrid state. That is why a high-level angel like Lucifer could fall so completely and be corrupted beyond recognition of anything that came from God. The evil that has decayed the once beautiful angel of God into the most horrific and hateful being of all time shows the extent that sin can have on a person.

Satan is the enemy of God, who has also made himself our adversary and is condemning us before the Father (Revelation 12:10). The enemy moves throughout the Earth seeking who he MAY devour (1st Peter 5:8) but, that is only if we give him an opening in our lives. That is why the Apostle Paul advised Christians to be vigilant and to put on God's full armor (Ephesians 6:11-18). Satan does not use any new tricks; the old ones still work on us, where he attacks us body, soul, and spirit, just as he tempted Jesus. First is always the flesh and comforts of this world, which can distract us from the purpose that God has for us. The second is to tempt our soul to seek after power and disconnect us from God through pride. The third is to discourage us from following God or to have us reject the priority of God outright so he can steal our personal focus. We do not need to fear because Jesus has overcome the enemy and all his powerful tricks and illusions (John 16:33; Hebrews 2:14-15).

There are in this world different kinds of spirits that are our enemies, which are mentioned in the Holy Bible. First are demonic spirits, which are the fallen angels that followed Satan (Matthew 12:43-45; 1st Peter 5:8; Revelation 16:14). Second, the evil spirits mentioned are the earthbound fallen ones from the Nephilim's destruction (Genesis 6:1-4, 1st John 4:1, Ephesians 6:10-12, Luke 10:19). The Nephilim are, of course, the children of the fallen Watcher Angels, and being only half-human, they cannot move on but are held on Earth until the day of judgment. One notable fact about the Nephilim was that they had six fingers and toes, aside from their gigantic size. They seemed to like the Samaria area, where there have been artifacts discovered with multiple fingers, more than a normal human (Samuel 21:20-21, 1st Chronicles 20:4-8, 1st Enoch 7:2-6).

This book was written to help Christians understand the wonders of salvation and the price God paid just to have us. With the examination of the Holy Bible's record of the strongmen listed throughout the Old and New Testaments. In reference to Jesus' statement about binding the strongman (Matthew 12:29; Mark 3:27; Luke 11:21-22) first before you can take the house, this refers to the Dominions, Principalities, Powers and Rulers of Darkness. The enemy has its own hierarchy to combat the faithful in this world, just like an army has generals, colonels, captains, and lieutenants that are assigned duties to fight their enemy.

The reader needs to prepare themselves to overcome our enemy by using God's provisions in combat with the enemy of this world so people can be saved, healed, and set free. This is not just a skirmish; it is all-out war, and its designs are for total annihilation. Our only hope is to trust in Jesus and be led by the Holy Spirit in order to be victorious. We must stand firm, as the Bible says in Ephesians 6:11-16, for God is with us (Deuteronomy 31:6, Isaiah 41:10, John 14:27) and trust in God's righteousness for our lives. Bless the holy name of Jesus, the risen Son of God and savior of the world.

Chapter Five

The Remnant

THE WORLD HAS always fought against those who follow God's ways because the world is controlled by evil and wants to stop God. No matter what the battles have been, those who were sidetracked by sin brought self-destruction upon themselves, but God has always saved a remnant to continue His ways (Romans 9:27). When Moses led the Israelis through the wilderness and they saw God's miracles for forty years, then tried to go back to Egypt after rebelling, God still saved the faithful few (Exodus 32:18). During the time of Noah, when God decided to destroy all the Nephilim, he still saved Noah and his family. God extended an invitation to the lost to repent and gave them plenty of time since it took Noah so long to build the Ark (Genesis 6:3-7). In the end, it was only Noah and his family that made it through.

Only after God dissolved a layer of our atmosphere and broke forth the fountains of the Earth did the people realize their missed opportunity. It says they were buying and selling like any other day, and that's the way it will be at the end too (Matthew 24:37-39). If you follow the up's and down's the Israelis had in the Promised Land, which is found in the books of Kings and Judges, you will also see that God always saved a remnant. Abraham was called out of the land of Ur, which is south of the Samaria area, so I believe he would be familiar with the Nephilim.

The Scriptures also mention the future after the rapture (1st Thessalonians 4:13-18), which is what we call the "taking up of the Christian believers" when Christ returns for His own. When this happens, the Holy Spirit will return to Heaven as well, and it says the people will do whatever enters their minds. Even after the final week of Daniel, known as "The Great Tribulations," God will still show mercy to those who had rejected Jesus, but it will cost them their physical lives. Martyrdom is a small price to pay for the salvation of your soul, since these people ignored God's warning before the rapture. God is always merciful and kind to those who repent of their sins and want to get right with God. There is a warning though: if you take the "Mark of the Beast," you have forfeited your salvation because that action means you have sided with the enemy (Revelation 13:11-18).

Several have speculated what the mark will be, but know this: the number will be 666, just like it is mentioned in the book of Revelation. In the original Greek manuscript, it stated "in" the forehead or back of the hand and not "on." I guess whoever translated it didn't think God knew his grammar very well. God always knows the right thing, because they have developed a chip they want to give everyone by implanting it under the skin (Revelation 13:16-17).

There is much controversy over the type of Mark, but let me give you a clue. The Hebrew language has a special built-in code; every letter has a numeric sequence, and that's where they believe the Bible code comes from. Translating the letter "**W**" into Hebrew is the letter "**Vav**," and its numeric sequence is "**6**," which means you would translate **WWW** as **666**. There is no doubt that the computer tie-in code will proceed with whatever information they use, just like you always see at https://www.com. If you take this **sub-dermal chip,** you will doom yourself to Hell, and there is no coming back from taking the Mark. Don't take the CHIP! If you find yourself left behind because you delayed accepting Jesus as your Lord and Savior, then you must pay attention to this or you will lose your last chance. For those left behind, it will be a horrible time, similar to the time for the Jews under Hitler's regime, which showed no mercy. The people at that time will become so bloodthirsty and calloused that they will be cheering when Christians are put to death by beheading.

If you look at how God kept saving a remnant of Jewish people throughout the Old Testament, it is a statement to us today about what God is doing for the whole human race. As previously mentioned, God, knowing everything, knew what was coming from the very beginning. This is why God made the statement to Satan about "The Seed" that was going to destroy him (Genesis 3:15). Satan has desperately been trying to stop that prophecy of God, which of course he could not stop God's word. In the storyline where God is saving a Jewish remnant to keep His word, it is a reflection of what He is doing for all humanity by saving those that will come to Him. Thus, this is the overall statement of the Holy Bible to humanity: God is willing to save the lost if they repent, and He will accept all that come.

This current dispensation of the world will be about six thousand years and the seventh thousand year will be when Christ reigns on Earth bringing it to the potential it always had the possibility to be. As of the date of this book, the Hebrew calendar year is 5783, which is nearing the end of this age. The other dispensations of Earth have had billions of years just like scientists have found out, but they don't understand God's plan for renewing this planet. In the age to come, after Jesus reigns for a thousand years and the final judgement is made by God, he will make a new heaven and earth (Revelation chapters 21 and 22). At this stage, we will be in our celestial bodies no longer effected by sin and we will not be hindering the Holy Spirit anymore. I say this because that is the only way we could properly judge angels, like it says in 1st Corinthians 6:3. There is no way we could do this if we were still subjected to the flesh. At the conclusion of this wonderous time of salvation, God will have made everything perfect again, and we will live with Him for all eternity.

Chapter Six

Working for Our Good

God's plan has always been to give us hope for our future where we live in freedom to worship God in spirit and truth (Jeremiah 29:11; John 4:24). The amazing thing is how God can use anything to bring good to us, even when the evil enemy attacks. God can turn it around for good for those who love God (Romans 8:28). When Jesus died on the cross, the veil in the Holy of Holies was torn, indicating that the price had been paid to make us right with God and that there were no longer any divisions between us (Matthew 27:51)! Jesus took our punishment and paid the price under the direction of God the Father to redeem all humankind (Genesis 22:13; John 1:29; Mark 15:6-15; Romans 5:8; Galatians 1:4). By doing so, Jesus took all of our sin-related curses and paid for them all at once (Genesis 3:17-18, Job

5:13-14, Isaiah 59:9-10, Mark 15:33, Galatians 3:13). Simultaneously, Jesus clothed us in His righteousness, allowing us to come boldly before the throne and become children of God (Isaiah 61:10; Mark 15:24; Hebrews 10:19). These three blessings are the main ones Jesus bought at the cross, but there are many other rewards too.

Jesus gave us access to Heaven and the Father (Mark 1:10, 10:38, Hebrews 10:19-22), defined the Holy Trinity for us (Ephesians 1:3-14), and redefined the Kingdom Powers forevermore (Genesis 3:5, Philippians 2:5-11). Jesus is now the focus of salvation, which was God's plan to reveal to humankind at the right time (Genesis 3:15, 1st Corinthians 2:2-5). This also initiated the New Covenant between man and God, whereby grace we are saved and not by the Law of Works (Jeremiah 31:31-34, Matthew 26:26-28, Ephesians 2:8-9). The marvelous good news of the gospel is that Jesus conquered sin and death for us so we can have eternal life with Him (1st Corinthians 15:54-55, Galatians 3:13, Colossians 2:14, 1st Peter 2:24).

The Enemy was also defeated and stripped of his power by Jesus, who reduced the powers of darkness to rubble, never to rise again (1st Corinthians 15:57, Ephesians 2:20-21, Colossians 2:13, 1st John 4:4). At the very end, when God has had His final say and has recreated the universe to perfection, the believers will marvel at the fallen enemy (Isaiah 14:16; Revelations 21:1-7). But for us now, we must fight the good fight of faith against the enemy's attacks and push forward the kingdom of God. As Jesus put it, we must carry our own personal cross through this world, proving we are following God; the race that Saint Paul quite often spoke about (2nd Timothy 4:7).

Taking up our own personal cross is every Christian's duty in service to God and the kingdom (Matthew 16:24, 2nd Corinthians 2:14-17, Galatians 2:20, Philippians 2:5-8). This is quite often a very difficult struggle to balance our lives with the ultimate goal of bringing the Gospel to the whole world. This world is contaminated by sin, and we have an enemy that wants us to fail because he hates everything about God's goodness (James 4:7). That is why the Christians of this world must endeavor to persevere no matter what the world throws at us. Part of the job of Christians is to bring peace, unity, and reconciliation to this world by letting Jesus shine through us (Ephesians 2:14; Colossians 1:20). Jesus warns us about being contaminated by this world and sin, stating in no uncertain terms how important it is to stay focused (Matthew 5:29; Luke 16:14-15). The lure of material wealth is one of the most dangerous attacks of the enemy and destroys many good Christians. In the parable of the rich man and the camel, Jesus emphasized how important it was not to get caught up in material wealth (Matthew 19:20-24; Luke 16:19-21; 1st Timothy 6:10).

The unfortunate misuse of preachers quoting the Old Testament scripture Malachi 3:10, claiming it is a command from God to tithe, but if you read the scripture, you can clearly see it is a challenge from God to prove Him on giving (2nd Corinthians 9:7). Jesus mentions that it is good to tithe (Luke 6:38, 11:42), yet He shows His resolve in the story about the widow and two mites (Luke 21:1-4). In the Old Testament, there are certain reasons God has the Israelis pay the tithe after God gives them great victories. It then became part of the religious sect to demand tithing as a law of God rather than an act of thanksgiving. This of course benefited the ones in charge, who made quite a good living on the gifts, and we still have preachers today who make profit off of the gospel (2nd Corinthians 11:13; Galatians 3:1-5; Philippians 1:15-18; Hebrews 10:38). If you are paying attention, you have seen the televangelists who keep pushing people to give them money and promise God will bless them. We have seen the fall of many of them because they were false teachers using the gospel to make money. Jesus paid for all things on the cross and annulled the rules of law and replaced them with grace (Hebrews 7:8-19; Colossians 2:14). Tithing, offering, and alms are three giving rituals, each with its own specific purpose. Never let anyone make you feel that it is compulsory to give; it is to be given from your heart in thanks for all God has done for us. The world cannot understand why we give or do charitable acts because they are foolish and cannot understand the things of God.

The world is blind and has a hardened heart, not allowing them to see the truths of God or understand the greatness of His ways (Jeremiah 5:21, 1st Corinthians 1:23, Mark 8:18). Only those called to God's purposes will find that God has called them out of this world (Habakkuk 1:2-4; Romans 8:28-30; 10:9-13). In the book of Revelation 20:15, it refers to "The Book of Life" (Revelation 3:5, 13:8, 20:12, Philippians 4:3, Romans 8:37-39), which holds all the names of the people who belong to God. You want to be found in this book (Luke 10:20), and God, who knows everything that will ever happen in all time, pre-wrote the names in that book before time existed. If you have accepted Jesus Christ as your personal Lord and Savior, you should know that God chose you first, making a way for you to find Him. God, who knows everyone's heart and intentions, allows you to come to Him, but for those He sees as sinfully corrupt and considered unworthy, he allows their hearts to be hardened, dooming themselves (Exodus 4:21, Deuteronomy 2:30, Joshua 11:20, Lamentations 3:65, John 12:40, Romans 9:18, 11:7, and 11:25).

There are many opportunities for us to succeed and fail

in this life, but we are the ones that make it happen. To believers, don't fall away from your first love of Jesus; do not tolerate anything coming between you and Jesus, which is idolatry; don't compromise the truth by listening to false teachers; stay pure in your heart and shun evil deeds; always remain obedient to God's ways; and do not allow yourself to become lukewarm in your beliefs by being influenced by this world (Revelation 2:4; 3:19). So, here's the warning: repent and turn away from your sinful ways, and come to Jesus, your Savior!

Chapter Seven

KEYS TO HIS PURPOSE

THE FIRST KEY point is that we are in the world but not of it; as passengers on this plane, you must understand that it is not our home but our journey, and we seek our home in heaven (John 17:6-19).

The second key point is that we are not to follow our own desires for secular survival and comfort, but rather our Heavenly Father's will to be done. God laid out His principles for all in His Word, and when we follow them, we will find the promised abundance. Just as Jesus taught us in His sample prayer in Matthew 6:9-13 and Luke 11:2-4. We must lose our personal desires to find true life by following God's purpose for our lives (Matthew 10:39; John 12:24-26).

The third key point is that God is alive and still in control; we have everything because of Him (Acts 17:29; Colossians 1:17). He blesses us in every aspect of our lives, and being like Him, we too speak words of life or <u>curses</u>. God gave us this power through Jesus (the Word of God); we must be careful what we say, speaking only blessings with positive direction (the Power of the Creative Word is in Us!) and NOT the negative as this fallen world has. What we say has the power to give or take away strength. Our actions follow what we say out of our mouths, so the response to this reality we must be very careful (Proverbs 18:21; Ephesians 4:29-32).

Key four is that we must learn to tap into the power of God through prayer and fasting (Isaiah 58:6), just as Jesus did. Jesus, the one and only son of God, rose from the dead in power and glory, but while He walked the earth, He too had to receive power from God through much prayer and fasting. Jesus left His deity behind when He came to Earth in the form of a human and set the example of how we can live a victorious life by staying in prayer and fasting. The preparation we need is done through prayer and fasting which is how we do God's will, giving us the divine wisdom and strength. We must stay connected to the Source of Holiness, which is the God of Heaven. This is the only way we can live a holy life when we are connected to God, the source of holiness (Matthew 4:1-17; 6:16-18, Luke 4:1-14, 1st Corinthians 7:5, 2nd Corinthians 6:4-10).

The Holy Spirit, the third person of the Trinity, will give us gifts to help us when we connect with God. This is referenced by the <u>nine gifts of the Holy Spirit</u> (1st Corinthians 12:5-11) and <u>the nine fruits of the Spirit</u> (Galatians 5:22-23, 1st Corinthians 13:4-13), which bring about love and maturity in the Spirit. This takes us to the next level, where we care about others as we do ourselves. You develop an acute awareness of others and their needs, furthering your sensible compassion for others. We must learn to connect to others as well as with God to fully mature as Christians, to walk as Jesus did, and to understand God's mission for us in this life (1st Corinthians 13:11-13).

Key six is when we reach this level of synchronists harmony with God and mature walk with Him, we are ready to expand our life mission to His ultimate level. As stated in Acts 2:17-18, this is where I believe believers see visions, dream dreams, and move in God's prophetic power. We must seek God's dream for our lives and not what we desire; God's will is better than anything we can think up. I believe we are in the *<u>end times, and the pouring out of the Holy Spirit</u>* is already occurring. Do not be afraid when you reach this level because it is God stretching you to your full potential for His glory (Genesis 37:5-8, Joel 2:28).

Key seven is that when we no longer obstruct the Holy Spirit, He can help us in our walk with God (1st Thessalonians 5:19, Ephesians 4:30). You can cultivate an intuition to know *what to do, where to go,* and the *mission at hand*. Engaging with the Holy Spirit allows you to flow in him, and incredible things can be accomplished. You will discover that you no longer have worldly desires or for its evil things (Ephesians 4:17-24).

Key eight is the reference in the scriptures to a time when "the church" will reach an intensity where they edify and encourage each other in love. This will be a prelude to what heaven will be like as we all love one another. We need each other for the encouragement we can give in this life to help others overcome this world (Romans 14:19, 15:2, 1st Corinthians 8:1, 2nd Corinthians 13:10, Ephesians 4:11-16, 1st Thessalonians 5:11, Acts 9:31). Jesus repeated the question to Peter, "Do you love me?" Then He stated, "Feed my sheep" (John 21:15-17). God's design for us was to be a family, and we would be together for all eternity (Ephesians 1:5; 5:1-21, Mark 12:30, John 3:6, Galatians 4:4).

Key nine is understanding the <u>direction God has for humanity</u> and the part we play in it. As we grow in *purity, spiritual fruits,* and *giving thanks,* we will be filled with the melody of God in our hearts. It is important to get to the place stated in Philippians 1:11 where we are filled with the fruits of righteousness. Communion with God is where unity is found in the body and where our strength lies. Whether we are discussing flesh or celestial life, the only good can be found by being connected to the God of the universe, the source of all good! Once we come together in the truth of God, there will be nothing that can prevail against it, not even the gates of hell! (Matthew 16:18; Ephesians 5:8-14; Proverbs 28:25-26)

JESUS IS THE: Way; Truth; Life; Lamb of God (sacrifice and sanctification); Savior; Resurrection; Word; Water of Life; Light; The Door; Only Begotten Loved One; Shepherd; High Priest; Rock; Bread of Life; Chief Cornerstone; Vine; Advocate; Lord of the Sabbath; Author and Finisher of our faith.

Chapter Eight

END TIMES

MANY PEOPLE WILL argue that we are not in the end times because several other events in human history, like the world wars, led people to think it was the end. As bad as those times were, the end times will be much worse, and only recently has the world seen a two-million-man army (Revelation 9:16-18) with the ability to dry up the Euphrates River where they could cross (Revelation 16:12). These two events have never happened before and are the precursors to the End Times of the world. China's army is not for defense; it is for conquering the world, and Turkey spent a fortune building the dam across the Euphrates River just for electrical power. China, North Korea, Turkey, and Russia all have oppressive governments that never allow their people freedom and even treat them like government property. This tactic is from Satan, whom those countries serve, seeking to do what the enemy wants to do: kill, steal, and destroy (John 10:10, Luke 22:31, 1st Peter 5:8). The man of sin cannot be revealed until the Church and Holy Spirit are removed from the world, marking the end of the gentile period (Daniel 12:1-2, 1st Thessalonians 4:17; 5:18, 1st Corinthians 15:51-53). In the very end times, it says Israel will have no friends, but America has always been there for them. However, if something were to happen to America where it lost its power or was destroyed, that could leave Israel with no one.

In recent decades, America's relationship with Israel has been strained from time to time, and if our country backs away from Israel, God will back away from us (Genesis 12:3). Once the gentile period is finished, the last week of Daniel can take place, which is referred to as the "Tribulation Period" (Daniel 9:24-27; Matthew 24:15-21; 2nd Thessalonians 2:4). On this timeline, we are at the very end, waiting for the rapture of the church, and then the final end begins. After the church and the Holy Spirit return to heaven, war will be brought against Israel by a military coalition of Russia and the Arab countries (Ezekiel 38:14-16). This war will be over quickly as God descends to defend Israel, where there will be a massive slaughter of the evil hosts.

Satan is always looking for a way to impede God's will

through his trickery and lies; this is where the Antichrist signs a peace treaty with Israel to give them a false sense of safety. Part of the treaty will be to rebuild the Holy Temple in Jerusalem as a sign of good faith to the Israeli people. Unknown to the Jewish people is that "the Man of Sin" (the Antichrist) will use the Holy Temple to declare to the world that he is god. This will happen in the second part of the Tribulation Period known as "The Great Tribulations" because God brings down massive judgments on the earth (Revelation 6:1-17; 8:1-9; 21). There will be pestilence and total financial collapse in all countries across the world.

As Satan fools the whole world with his deceptions, the sin-controlled world's governments give over their authority to the Antichrist to rule the world. This is where the one world government comes into play and the "Mark of the Beast" is forced on everyone (Revelation 13:16-17). In a previous chapter, I discussed the mark and emphasized the importance of not accepting the chip, which contains the Mark of the Beast. Now, there is war in heaven, where the Archangel Michael casts Satan down to earth as he is defeated in heaven (Revelation 12:7-12). At this time, Satan knows his time is short and is very agitated with great anger! The Antichrist now enters the Holy Temple in Jerusalem and sits on the Mercy Seat of God, declaring he is god (Matthew 24:15-21).

Finally, the Jewish people wake up and see this is the time of "the abomination of desolation," and they instinctively know to flee Israel. God will save one hundred forty-four thousand Jewish people, twelve thousand from each tribe (Revelation 7:4-8), who will finally realize that Jesus (Yeshua) was the Christ. These will be the great evangelists of the day, traveling the globe and leading people to Christ. They will never take the mark of the beast and will be hunted by the Antichrist to destroy them. There will be two witnesses that God will send that will wield great power against the Antichrist and the Beast; some believe these are none other than Enoch and Elijah (Revelation 11:3).

The scripture refers to the fall of Babylon, which happens in one hour and seems to be the result of a nuclear attack. The Bible describes how the world is in awe and mourning the loss of Babylon, even weeping for their demise. Even refers to all the vendors who made a lot of money selling to Babylon and are now in anguish because they have no one to buy their products (Revelation 18:8-10). Babylon was slated to have unparalleled wealth and prosperity but was judged as the city that allowed debauchery, idolatry, sorcery, sexual immorality, and every other sort of unholy abomination. Sounds a lot like America, doesn't it?

Then it seems like the Antichrist and the Beast get the

upper hand when they are able to murder God's two witnesses. Their bodies are left in the streets where they were murdered; they are not buried, and people are celebrating that they are dead. It says people were even giving gifts to each other like we do for Christmas (Revelation 11:7-10) because they were so happy these men of God were dead. Can you imagine how people of the time are to be able to jeer at such a sight? You have to keep in mind that, at this time, the Holy Spirit, who convicts us of sin, has already returned to Heaven.

Of course, God has the last laugh because He is over life and death, raising the two witnesses back to life in front of the whole world (Revelation 11:11-13). This would indicate they were televising this situation, and God used it to bring glory to Himself. As I've stated in previous chapters, God goes in circles around the enemy and his plans to thwart God's purposes. It is at this time that God raises the witnesses not only back to life but also takes them up into heaven, just like Jesus left before the apostles.

The enemy knows his time is short and gathers the world's armies together to fight God, which is referred to as the Battle of Armageddon (Revelation 16:13-16). This is the foolishness of sin; Satan is still blindly thinking he can win against God. Humans may be foolish enough to believe they can defeat God, but a previous angel of God with the knowledge he possesses? The corruption of sin is absolute and brings about utter destruction, even for those that once had great knowledge and power.

Now comes the glorious appearing of Jesus the Christ, which is something humankind has been waiting for in anticipation for thousands of years. This is where Jesus comes in His full majesty and power to put down all the enemies of God (Matthew 24:27; Revelation 19:11-20). When Jesus lands, it will be spectacular to see the power He wields on Earth (Zechariah 14:3-9). With earthquakes and splitting mountains, it will be huge beyond anything we have ever seen. Jesus will put down the armies of evil once and for all, never to rise again, and war will cease throughout the world (Psalm 46:9-10). After everything is made right by Jesus, war won't even be practiced anymore, and weapons will be turned into plowshares (Isaiah 2:4).

As we approach the year 7000 of this compensation of the Earth, God demonstrates that only He can rule righteously. During the thousand-year reign of Christ, there will be great prosperity, peace, and justice, but even after Jesus shows humans how it should be, there are still those that reject Him?

The New Heaven and Earth are described in the last two chapters of The Book of Revelations, which are chapters twenty-one and twenty-two. This is where God makes everything new after burning it up with fire, and the New Earth will not have an ocean. I believe God required more land for all of the believers who will live with Him there. No more death, pain, or suffering will be on this new earth, and it says God will wipe away every tear. God will live among us, as He has always desired. There will be a New City of God with huge proportions that will come down and land from space, where only the Redeemed can live. It mentions that the Tabernacle of God will come down from heaven and be on this new earth. No sun will be needed because God's glory will light up the Earth and there will be no more night. The River of Life will be there for all to drink freely, and the Trees of Life will be there for all to pick the fruit all year. We will be marked by God with His name on our foreheads, declaring we belong to Him forevermore!

Chapter Nine

CONCLUSION

IN CONCLUSION OF all the points of God's great salvation plan, if you have read everything thus far, you will have noticed that I don't use fluff in my writing. I stick to the subject at hand, presenting the truths that are the most relevant to the points I have been making. I gave the reference scriptures I used to present the truth as I see it, and I want my readers to fact-check me! My desire is that all in the church seek knowledge for themselves without waiting on someone else to tell them what to believe (2nd Timothy 2:15). There have been many false teachings throughout the centuries, like the Gnostic system that developed from human understanding rather than God's written word (Colossians 2:8-23, 1st Timothy 1:4, 2nd Timothy 2:16-19, Titus 1:10-16). Saint Paul also reminds us that we were delivered from sin and that we now live in the holiness that Jesus purchased for us (Romans 6:1-11, 1st John 3:4-10).

To reiterate, we are in the last days and must be very watchful of the deceit of our day since the enemy is working overtime to hinder everything of God (2nd Thessalonians 2:1-12). Some science tries to explain away the faith of the scriptures, but nevertheless, God's word stands true. We have an enemy, which is also the enemy of God, attempting to destroy everything that is good. We know that our flesh is weak and our mental capacity is limited (Matthew 26:41, 2nd Corinthians 12:7), so we must stay in prayer to stay connected to God, who is our strength.

God has gone through a lot to bring salvation to humankind by developing this storyline of angels and the falls and using it to bring about a higher level of spiritual being. His design was to create children for himself, and we would live with him forever in the New Heavens and Earth! Remember that time has no effect on God because He exists outside of our known existence and can take as long as He wants to accomplish His will. This is the amazing story behind salvation: God put so much into it at a very high price, and yet, love still flows from God in every moment of our existence.

The jealousy of the enemy to destroy what is precious to God because Satan was unable to rise to the heights he wanted is full of his utter contempt for humanity. All the deception and lies Satan has brought about to destroy humanity are the result of his overinflated self-worth, vanity and pride which border on insanity. Nonetheless, Jesus destroyed all of the enemy's works in one action at the cross, which had been predicted for thousands of years and that the enemy could never stop. How marvelous is our God! Loving, kind, patient, and ever doting toward the humble of His creation, which He loves with all His life?

The meaning of salvation is that God has been planning this for thousands of years with a very intricate and complex strategy, which cost God immensely to bring salvation to us! God has played this symphony of salvation from the beginning of time, looking forward to the day it would be completed and we could live together with Him in Heaven forever.

To God be the glory; you are worthy, O Lord, to receive glory, honor, and power; for you created all things, and they exist and were created because of your will; let the entire creation resound; Holy, Holy, Holy, Lord God Almighty, who was and is and is to come, praise God forevermore! Amen and amen.

CPSIA information can be obtained
at www.ICGtesting.com
Printed in the USA
BVHW071432160223
658647BV00014B/894